Introduction

I am Brittany Gunderson. I have a few mental disorders from being in abusive relationships.

One of my disorders is Agoraphobia. In this book, I will explain what agoraphobia is and how it feels, techniques I used to get better, and how I managed to get on stage. I am currently 26 years old and I've had agoraphobia since I was 18.

Another disorder I have is Depression. I've had depression since I was 17. I will discuss what depression is, what it feels like, and how I cope.

I have Post-Traumatic Stress Disorder from abusive relationships. I've had it since I was 18. I will explain PTSD and how it feels. I will discuss how I cope with it as well.

Through my depression, pain, and hardship, I have learned how to be happy. You can, too. I will show you what I've done and hopefully inspire you to make changes in your own life.

I am a mother, a daughter, a girlfriend, an author, a youth group leader, and a domestic violence advocate. I have come a very long way in the past year. I am hoping to help you become better, happier, and healthier in dealing with your own fears, agoraphobia, depression, codependency, and Post- Traumatic Stress Disorder.

Part One- Agoraphobia

From Agoraphobia To The Stage

Chapter One:

What Is Agoraphobia

Agoraphobia is the fear of leaving your home, being out in public places, and the fear of having a panic attack in public. My agoraphobia contains panic attacks. Some people with agoraphobia do not have panic attacks.

There are different levels of agoraphobia. Some people never leave their home for anything. They have others do everything for them. Some people can leave with someone close that they trust. Some people avoid certain places, but are okay in other places. There are various reasons why people get agoraphobic.

The reason I have agoraphobia is because of being in abusive relationships. My most abusive ex would not allow me to leave the house or I would get shaken, hit, or choked. I got very comfortable staying home.

I, then, decided that the public wasn't safe. I was afraid that I would run into an abusive ex. Any of them could harm me in public because they would while I was with them. I learned that these fears were unrealistic because if they approached me, they would most likely leave me alone. If they didn't, help would be right there. After learning that, I eased up a little about going places.

When I walk to my church, I wear my headphones. I listen to music to help keep me calm. I can only go to the store with my boyfriend. I do currently have a slight case of agoraphobia. The difference between now and a year ago is, I go places and do new things despite the fear.

Agoraphobia causes me to have a strong sense of panic whenever I go to open my home door. I literally have to take deep breaths and force myself to leave, but I do. I have occasionally turned to my boyfriend and said, "I am afraid."

My boyfriend reassures me that I'll be okay and he is only a phone call away. I put on a bold, brave face and open the door.

Agoraphobia stems from a fear of something that happened outside of your home, or something that could happen. I am hyper-vigilant and often walk with my fists clenched. I am ready to fight off an attacker. This is a symptom of my Post-Traumatic Stress Disorder as well. Music helps this as I said before.

Agoraphobia is a branch of panic disorders. I have a lot of anxiety and I panic a lot. I am a worrier. I worry about getting hurt in public, seeing an abusive ex, or people staring at me.

I used to walk with my head down. No one was in my existence. I didn't notice people who passed by me or cars. They simply didn't exist to me. I could go all day with out seeing a single person, but they were really there.

My therapist said that what I was doing was a coping mechanism that helped me at the time. I could literally erase people and cars from my mind and not see them. I got very good at this.

Chapter 2:

The First Step

In January of 2014, I moved from Maryland to Delaware. Most of my family is in Maryland. This was a big step for me. All of a sudden, I was alone with my children and my current boyfriend. Every one I relied on were far away and I don't drive, yet.

I walk everywhere and I needed to explore my new town. I needed to find the library, local playground, and stores. I took my boyfriend with me every where.

My boyfriend is more outgoing than I was at the time. He would say, "Hey, how are you?" to every one that we passed on the sidewalk.

This behavior of his upset me greatly. You see, I was so used to not noticing people that I passed and he was forcing them into my awareness. I would have to accept their existence if he was speaking to them. Plus, I wanted to know who he was talking to. So I had to start noticing people and bring them into my awareness.

That, I believe, was my first step toward getting better. If you walk around oblivious to the world and the people in it, start letting them into your awareness and acknowledge their existence.

The second part of the first step is a little more difficult. It was extremely hard for me in the beginning. After about four months of acknowledging people, I began to say, "Hey, how are you?" when I passed by them. This took a few steps to accomplish. At first, I would do a little head nod if they spoke to me first. Then, I would say, "Hey." Finally, I was able to get the whole sentence out.

This is truly beneficial for agoraphobia as well as social anxiety. Force yourself to say a simple sentence to every one you come close to through out the day. Now, I am to the point where I can smile as I say, "Hey, how are you?"

It takes time and persistence to do this. You must resist the fear and don't shut yourself down. It's scary reaching out to other people, but it is very rewarding. I can do this as long as I am with my boyfriend. I'm still working on being by myself. I use headphones and that keeps me from socializing while walking alone. I do wave though and nod while acknowledging their existence.

It took me about six months to get comfortable doing that. I had help from my therapist and my boyfriend to get to that point. Support is very important in recovering.

Chapter Three:

The Second Step

I highly recommend therapy. If you are trying to do this on your own, it will be really hard. I suffered from all of my disorders for seven years without medication. I had a therapist alone for four of those seven years.

I was very afraid to try medication. I had irrational fears. My biggest fear was that I wouldn't be "me" anymore. I wouldn't know how to act to not being depressed and emotional. I decided to give medication a try when I found out my therapist was on medication and it didn't change him.

I was so afraid that I would be different or not have any emotions. This is not true. I still get sad, angry, upset, and have "off" days where I just lay around on the couch. I am also able to be happy and joyful. I still cry sometimes. Medication just makes you feel better and helps greatly. I recommend trying it. If you really don't like it, try a different one. Eventually, you and your psychiatrist will find the right medicine or right combination of medicine.

Once I got comfortable on my medicine, I noticed that I had more calm and better days than not. I didn't snap so quickly. I was more in control of my actions and emotions.

I read many self-help books once I was medicated and I started learning new thought processes. I changed my negative thoughts into realistic thoughts. We tend to have anxiety provoking thoughts that are negative and don't hold evidence. We need to challenge the evidence of our thoughts.

My thoughts that trigger my agoraphobia are: I'm going to get attacked; Something bad will happen; People are going to stare at me; My social anxiety; I'll stumble over my words. These thoughts are negative and anxiety provoking.

Where is the evidence? How can I make these thoughts realistic? I'll show you how.

A thought record keeps track of and helps you change your thoughts. On a horizontal paper, make seven columns.

The first column is labeled: Situation. Who was involved? What happened? Where were you? When did this event happen?

Ex. Today at home talking about my son's first day of school in one week, I got panicky thinking about the bus stop.

The second column is labeled: Moods. Here you write down the moods, emotions, and physical feelings you are experiencing and rate them from 1-100%.

Ex. Anxious 90%

Panic 100%

Worry 50%

Dry Mouth 100%

Difficulty Breathing 90%

Racing Heart 80%

The third column is for your Automatic Thoughts. Automatic thoughts are the thoughts that come to you and they are usually negative.

Ex. I have to stand at the bus stop and wait with strangers.

I can't do this.

Groups humiliate me.

I'm having a panic attack.

Circle your trigger thoughts. The ones that cause the most turmoil within you.

The fourth column is: Supporting Evidence. What is true about these automatic thoughts?

Ex. Kids live here

If my son runs around or doesn't listen to me, I will feel humiliated.

The fifth column is: Contradicting Evidence. What about your automatic thoughts are not one hundred per cent true all of the time?

Ex. The kids may not go to the same school.

I've waited last year in a small group at the bus stop and I   was fine.

The sixth column is: Realistic Thoughts. These thoughts are a combination of your supporting evidence and your contradicting evidence. Rate how much you believe in each one on a scale of 1-100%

Ex. Kids live here but they may not go to my son's school.   70%

I have been humiliated at the bus stop before and I   survived the embarrassment. 100%

This year my son is older and listens better than last year.

90%

The final column is your mood now. How do you feel now that your thoughts have went from negative to realistic? Rate the same moods again that you wrote in column two.

Ex. Anxious 40%

Panic 10%

Worry 5%

All physical symptoms returned to normal.

I hope you can understand how to do a thought record. A full example follows:

Situation:

I am at the store and I get overwhelmed and cry   because my son runs off.

Moods:

Anxious 90%

Overwhelmed 100%

Embarrased 90%

Auto-Thoughts:

I can't control my son.

People are staring.

I'm a bad mother.

I want to be home.

This is humiliating.

Supporting evidence:

My son ran off.

People are looking at me.

Contradicting evidence:

They aren't staring.

I'm a good mother for many reasons.

Realistic Thoughts:

Although my son ran off, that doesn't mean
I am a   bad mother. 100%

People look and then go on about their business. 90%

Mood now:

Anxious 50%

Overwhelmed 40%

Embarrased 30%

I highly recommend reading Mind Over Mood by Dennis Greenberger for further reading on changing negative thoughts, beliefs, and views. This is called Cognitive Behavioral Therapy.

Chapter Four:

The Third Step

After I got used to talking to random people, taking medication, and changing my thoughts to more realistic thoughts, I joined a mental health support group.

I joined the group in February of 2015. So, I had a year of getting used to acknowledging people, six months of medication, and many months of thought changing first.

I remember being shaky and scared on the ride there. I tried to keep my thoughts in check and keep them realistic. I was very nervous. It helped that I had a comedian driver who kept me laughing the whole way.

So, in my support group, every one gets one minute to talk about their life. I was shaking from head to toe when it was my turn. My mouth was dry and my heart was racing. I stared hard at the table as I croaked out my words. I explained my disorders and that it was almost a miracle that I was there.

I got a lot of supportive comments and praises for being there. I was put at ease and tried hard to relax for the rest of the time. I went every week for almost eight months. Over time, my confidence raised. Now, I am able to smile, make eye contact, and talk normal in my group.

I recommend joining a support group near you. You will see that you are not alone, you will have support, and you will get comfortable over time. I was nervous for the first four weeks before I got more comfortable.

Without my support group, I would not have made it this far. They really pulled me out of my shell and helped me become more assertive and confident.

Chapter Five:

Church

After my first three steps, I decided to go to church one day. I sat all the way in the very back. I dreaded having to meet and greet everyone by shaking hands. It caused a lot of anxiety within me.

Over the next few weeks, I built up a smile with the handshakes and good mornings. My church has a Praise and Worship Team which is a band that leads the congregation in song. Four months after I started going to my church, I decided that I needed to be on the Praise Team and sing.

This was a huge, scary step for me. I had to sing alone for an audition and boy was my singing shaky. Despite that, they allowed me to join. I spent four weeks off stage, practicing with them. Finally, my day to be on stage came. My friend offered me a lot of advice that morning. Don't look at the people was the main one she shared.

I didn't look at the crowd of 200 plus people at all. I focused on the songs and kept my thoughts blank. Act as if is a very important part of this. I learned that if you act as if you already are accomplished, then you can do it. That day I acted as if I knew what I was doing and that I had done it thousands of times and that really helped me.

Over the next month, I was eventually able to look out at the crowd and not be scared at all. I was very confident and happy up there.

Along with Praise and Worship, I joined Fusion. Fusion is the youth ministry. I became a youth leader. I went on one trip, camping for a night. I was very nervous on the bus there, but I kept my thoughts positive. I had a great time!

Chapter Six:

Hiccup

I had a slight hiccup in my recovery. I was supposed to go to Ocean City for a weekend with Fusion. We were going to take 40-60 of our church kids and meet up with about 4,000 other kids. I was overwhelmed.

I made my list of things to take and I started panicking. I went into a full blown panic attack. I was rocking with anxiety for hours. I had trouble breathing and kept crying.

I decided to not go. I just wasn't ready for that. My thoughts were all negative and catastrophic. Things are going to go wrong. We are going to lose track of our kids. I'm scared to death. All of those were triggering my panic. Lo and behold, they all did fine on the trip. No problems or anything.

I missed out on a very exciting trip due to my panic and agoraphobia. I regret it. There is next year, however, and I will be ready then.

Not only did I panic and miss the trip, I went into a mental relapse and had to take off everything for a month. I quit Fusion and Praise Team. I kept my writing group, however. Writing Group is a great group of writers and I look forward to it every week at church.

At any rate, I did work back up in a month to go back to church. I joined Fusion again. I wanted to join Praise Team, but they got too full. I am excited for the upcoming Fusion events.

To combat my fear, I use excitement. The more I am excited and looking forward to doing something, the less afraid I am.

Chapter Seven:

The Next Step

While I was taking a break from church, I put my volunteer application in to a domestic violence organization. I will be speaking to groups of people about domestic violence awareness.

I am looking forward to this experience. I want to become a public speaker and this is a great way to do so. I will be discussing a cause that is very close to my heart and helping others. I am ready for this and I hope to change lives.

I may be shaky at first, but I will gain confidence and self-esteem along the way. I take baby steps and I get a lot accomplished one step at a time.

Chapter Eight:

The Bad Part

I still can't go to the store by myself. I have to have my boyfriend with me. This is why. It happened about six months ago. One morning, I needed to go get breakfast for my family. I didn't want to get everyone dressed to go. I figured with it being seven in the morning, I would be fine.

I didn't have my headphones in that day. I walk a little path through a meadow which is a short cut to the store. I heard shuffling behind me. I turned around, but they were further behind me and I couldn't see them. I continued walking.

As I came to the exit of the meadow, he caught up to me. I noticed that he wasn't familiar and I never saw him before. He was a black man about my age. He said, "Hi."

I responded as I was walking. He said, "I just got off work."

"Ok," I said, quickening my pace. I had to go around the side of the shopping center to the front to go in the store.

He backed off and I entered the store. I got the few items and left. He was waiting for me on the side of the building.

He asked me, "Do you have a boyfriend?"

I said, "Yes, I do." That was when he grabbed my bottom. "Don't touch me," I growled. "You don't touch me!"

He put his hands up and apologised saying, "I just wanted to touch."

I said, "Well, don't." By now I was walking fast with him right behind me. I entered the meadow. I placed my hand into my pocket only to realize my phone wasn't there. I had left it at home. He got behind me again. He said vulgar things to me. He followed me on the meadow path . Before we got into the camera's view, he backed off and went the opposite direction.

I hurried across the parking lot of my development and quickly got in my home. I locked the door and started balling.

My boyfriend asked me what happened and I explained. He looked for him out the window but couldn't see him any where.

A few days later, I was walking to the store with my boyfriend and saw that guy. He saw me point at him and tell my boyfriend. That's the last time I've seen him. I assume he was just visiting the area.

I have to be honest with myself, it was one scary event in the two years that I've lived here. With that knowledge, I still am afraid to go to the store alone. Maybe one day I can work on that and be able to.

Part Two- Depression

From Depression To Stability

Chapter One:

What Is Depression

Depression is a hard disorder to cope with. You feel worthless, hopeless, and you don't feel like doing anything. Depression is often a chemical imbalance in the brain and can be helped with therapy, medication, and cognitive therapy.

When you have depression, you feel stuck. You feel miserable and lost. It can be a scary feeling. I've had depression since I was seventeen. It was triggered by my parent's divorce and the death of a friend.

I didn't want to eat, do homework, or even have fun. I just laid around and moped. I had insomnia as well. The inability to sleep made my depression so much worse.

Before I got on medicine, my days were usually bad and moody. I'd lay around, argue, and wallow in pain. I felt lonely, worthless, and had no hope at all. Now, I have very few days like that.

Depression is like a deep hole that you can't get out of. Happiness is relatively non-existent. It feels just like giving up. You literally give up on everything in life, including life itself. Every task seems daunting and very overwhelming. You spend the majority of your time laying around.

Chapter Two:

An Off Day

Even once you are on medicine, you will have an off day occasionally. An off day is when you are depressed and lay around. That is okay to do, sometimes. You won't be happy all of the time and that's okay, too.

We need a time to ourselves to lay around and wallow. Sometimes, we take on too much and just need to recuperate. Give yourself permission to lay around and do nothing once in a while. When this becomes your daily life, then you do need to get help. Occasionally it is fine, but all the time is not.

Take time for you. Enjoy a nice, hot beverage or a steamy bubble bath. Curl up and read a good book. I do these things when my mood gets a little low. They help prevent an off day from happening.

I still get off days occasionally. I still cry and get scared. We are not meant to be happy and content all of the time, and that's okay.

Chapter Three:

Symptoms

Lasting sadness, self-hate, irritability, loss of interest, hopelessness, anxiety, isolation, lack of energy, changes in sleep habits, loss or increase of appetite, and suicidal tendencies are a few symptoms of depression.

I have had them all at one point or another. They are not easy to live with. There would be weeks where I just stayed in bed and never got up except to use the bathroom.

Depression takes its toll on your whole body. You will feel defeated and tired all the time. Sadness is your main emotion. You start to hate who you are and lose all confidence and self-esteem. You don't want to do activities that you once enjoyed.

Everything seems hopeless. But, the truth is, there is help for you. There is medication and therapy. You don't have to suffer any longer.

Chapter Four:

How I Cope

I use many different techniques to help me feel better. I enjoy nature walks, meditation, guided imagery, and little things. I love hot tea and warm baths. I love to dance. I exercise to combat the energy drain.

Guided imagery works great for me. I usually use peaceful place imagery. I sit and take deep breaths until I feel relaxed and then envision a beautiful, calm, quiet place. I think about this place until I feel calm and relaxed.

I read uplifting and inspirational books. I love to color because it helps me quiet my mind.

When I get real low down, I allow myself an off day and then I feel fine the next day. I get involved with causes, volunteering, and my church. By doing so, I keep busy and keep sad thoughts at bay.

I do positive thinking exercises, mirror work, and self-esteem exercises. I tell myself, "I love you" while looking in the mirror. It truly helps.

I love to write out my feelings in a journal. All the depression seems to seep out of me as ink. I also use my blog a lot.

Chapter Five:

The Next Step

I am currently working on confidence, self-esteem, and assertiveness training. I have trouble looking people in the eye. I have trouble holding a bold posture. I am working on this with my therapist. We believe that if I get better at these things, I will be less depressed and more in control of myself.

I plan to learn how to have serious conversations without being meek and nervous. I plan to not back down to someone of power and confidence.

There will be a day when I am confident, assertive, and have high self-esteem. These are the next steps.

Part Three- Post-Traumatic Stress Disorder

From PTSD To Calm

Chapter One:

What Is PTSD

Post-Traumatic Stress Disorder (PTSD) is a reaction to an intensely stressful event. Some people get it from going to war, rape, car accidents, and abuse.

Mine is from abusive relationships. I flinch a lot. I startle easily. Flashbacks of the period of abuse comes back to me and I forget that I am really okay.

During my abusive relationship, I was abused mentally, physically, emotionally, and sexually. Abuse has very long, lasting effects within you.

You will have flashbacks, startle easily, and have high adrenaline all the time. Different things that remind you of the stressful time will cause flashbacks. These are called triggers.

There is no cure for PTSD. All you can do is train yourself to be more calm.

Chapter Two:

How I Cope

It helps greatly that I am in a healthy relationship now. I don't have to worry about getting hit or controlled by the man I am currently with. He treats me with respect and encourages me. He makes me feel like I am worth something.

I am hyper-vigilant so I use headphones to help keep me calm while walking. I stay ready for anything. If I don't use headphones, every sound sets off my panic.

I avoid triggers that will set off my symptoms of PTSD. I use meditation to help keep me calm. I have also desensitized a few of my triggers by owning them back and not linking them to that time frame. Certain smells, tastes, and sounds get to me, however.

I keep my thoughts realistic and calm the majority of the time. This helps greatly. I still get scared easily, but over time my startle reflex should get better. It's so easy to startle me.

Chapter Three:

Deep Breathing

When I feel extra panicky or tense, I do a deep breathing activity. You can easily do this activity yourself.

Place your hand over your belly and breath deeply through your nose. Feel your abdomen fully expand and then slowly release the breath through your mouth.

When you breathe through your nose, more air gets to your lungs. When you breathe in through your mouth, a lot of the oxygen goes to your stomach.

You can do this any time you feel overwhelmed and it will instantly calm you. Breathe in at least ten deep, powerful breaths and release them slowly for ultimate results.

You will feel better fast. Keep your thoughts realistic and positive while you do deep breathing exercises.

Chapter Four:

The Next Step

The next step would be to remain calm in stressful situations. To do so, I must keep my thoughts realistic. Not everyone is out to get me. I'm going to be safe.

I need to continue using guided imagery and meditation to train my body to be calm. My body is used to being tense and alert. My adrenaline is always higher than most people. I'm constantly ready to run or fight. By meditating, I help my body learn how to be calm.

I need to practice desensitization by imagining staying calm in a stressful situation. Then, I have to actually stay calm during a stressful situation. These are all being worked on currently.

These techniques are also valuable for anxiety and social anxiety as well. I have been working on eliminating my own anxiety and social fears. It starts with changing my thoughts and training my body to be calm.

Part Four- Codependency

From Codependency To Independant

Chapter One:

What is Codependency

Codependancy is an unhealthy dependance on a person for approval and identity. I used to have codependency very badly. I couldn't do anything without permission first. I couldn't make my own decisions. I had to be told what to do.

I still have issues making decisions, but not as bad. Instead of saying, "Can I...?", I say, "Do you mind if....?"

By doing that, you aren't asking for permission, you are just making sure it won't clash with your partner's plans.

There was a time when I couldn't eat dinner if my boyfriend didn't eat exactly the same thing and at the same time as me. I couldn't go anywhere with out him. When he moved, I moved. That's how it was.

Things are different now. I have my own life apart from him. I have my own, unique identities.

Such as, author, team leader, and domestic violence advocate. I go to church and do all my activities apart from him. This took a long time to achieve.

Now, I can eat without him and something other than what he is eating. I used to get codependent on other people as well. I was codependent on my old therapist at one point.

They say codependency is unhealthy. I don't quite agree with that. I feel that I am more in tune with my boyfriend than most relationships can say. We don't have arguments, but we discuss big issues when and if they ever arise. I am more caring of how he would feel.

What they said was unhealthy is when I lost my own identity. I didn't have an identity other than "mother" for nearly a decade. I was always asking permission or having someone else make my decisions for me. That, I agree, is unhealthy.

Chapter Two:

Symptoms

The symptoms of codependency are inability to be alone, needing reassurance, needing permission, low self-worth, tumultuous relationships, and losing one's identity.

When you are no longer separate people, but move as one person in a unhealthy way then you may be codependent. An unhealthy way is when you put your dreams, choices, and desires completely off to do what your partner wants all of the time.

You need to have your own identity and do what your heart desires. Be who you choose to be and want to be. It's vital to our existence.

There are many ways to change being codependent and you can try a few of them.

Chapter Three:

How I Changed

I started making my own decisions and I felt very guilty at first. It helped that I have a boyfriend who isn't controlling. My exes were all very controlling and abusive.

I would make simple decisions first. For example, deciding what to eat for dinner, to go to the library that day, or visit the playground with the kids.

I eventually got comfortable making little decisions. At first, I would always ask my current boyfriend for permission and he would repeatedly tell me, "I'm not your boss. Do whatever you want."

That gave me permission to make my own choices in my day. I started to make more decisions for myself.

One day, I decided I wanted to cut my hair short and dye it. Because I could, I did. One month it was burgundy, the next was blue, and the next was emerald green. I had my fun and eventually dyed it back to its normal dark brown.

I did not make my own decision to go to a support group. I was encouraged to go by one of my therapists. I'm so glad I did. I made bigger decisions after that. I chose to go to church, become active in the church, and apply for the domestic violence awareness team.

Being in charge of your life is important for happiness and well-being. When you are controlled to the point where you can't make decisions and you get free, you need to learn that it is okay to have choices and make decisions. It truly is okay. I had to learn that.

The main thing I did was just start doing and stop asking for permission.

Chapter Four:

The Next Step

The next step in my recovery is to not feel so guilty of my decisions and to trust myself to make the right decision on my own.

I have a lack of faith in my choices and decisions, but I am getting better about that. I know that mistakes may be made, but you can always learn from them. For me, missing the Ocean City Trip with Fusion was a big mistake. I learned to never give in to my panic and agoraphobia again because I'll regret it.

I know deep down that I will make good decisions for me at any given time. I know you will, too. We have gut feelings and they need to be addressed.

I am becoming more independent than I have ever been in my whole life. I will be getting my license this year and that will definitely help my independence. I won't have to rely on people to take my where I need to go. That will be a huge accomplishment for me.

Part Five-

Other Lifestyle Changes

Chapter One:

Nutrition

Nutrition is vital to feeling better and being more healthy. When you eat greasy, surgery, or fatty foods, you feel more bloated, down, and sluggish.

Be sure to eat fresh fruits and vegetables, lean protein, and whole grain foods. Bake your chicken rather than fry it. What goes into your body effects greatly how your body feels.

Make healthy choices and be mindful. Indulge in sweets and chips sparingly. You will feel so much better after eliminating unhealthy foods and beverages.

Chapter Two:

Exercise

Exercise makes you feel better because it creates endorphins through your body which make you feel good. You will combat the energy drain of depression.

I recommend exercising at least twenty minutes a day. More is better, but twenty is good to start out with. You have many options. You can buy an exercise DVD to go along with, you can join a gym, Yoga, Pilates, or weight lifting are great ideas.

Dancing, bicycling, swimming, and roller skating are fun ways to exercise. Be creative with your exercise routine. Just walking around your town is beneficial to your health.

Chapter Three:

Personal Hygiene

Personal hygiene is important for happiness. When you go a long time without a shower and your hair gets greasy, you tend to suffer in the self-esteem department. Sometimes people are so depressed that they neglect their hygiene.

Brush your teeth and you will feel refreshed and more confident when speaking to people. Make yourself feel better by simply taking care of your body in every way.

Pamper yourself with nice, calming, bubble baths. They do wonders for the soul. You will have more self-esteem when you bathe, shower, and brush your teeth.

When you have more self-esteem, you are more likely to reach out to people, smile, and have more confidence.

Chapter Four:

Daily Relaxation

You need time to reflect daily. You can use meditation, prayer, guided imagery, or reflection to obtain relaxation.

Meditation is simply quieting your mind and focusing on your breathing. When a thought comes, simply acknowledge it and let it pass.

Prayer is important for your spirituality. You can spend time praying and being close to God.

Guided Imagery is relaxing and focusing on a particular image. You can do peaceful place imagery or floating on a cloud imagery. You can easily find these online.

Reflection is focusing on how far you have come already, who you are, and who you want to become. You will discover your deepest dreams and desires when you reflect often.

Be sure to sit in a quiet room or use relaxing music. Don't try to relax when you have a lot of distractions going on.

Chapter Five:

Eliminate Negativity

There are many forms of negativity in this world. There are negative people who try to drag you down with them. There are our own negative thoughts.

We need to have a negativity cleaning. Distance yourself from negative people by limiting your exposure to them. Don't allow what they say to get to you and manifest within your head.

Love these negative people from a distance to keep your well-being. You don't have to see them often and you definitely don't have to give in to the negativity they say.

In some cases, you may be able to simply cut them out completely. Don't associate with them any more if you can. They are harmful to your well-being.

Chapter Six:

Eliminate Bad Habits

Smoking, drinking, and doing drugs are all bad habits that ultimately make you feel worse even though you think they help.

Smoking can cause many health problems. You can have difficulty breathing and cough a lot. At its worst, you can develop lung cancer or emphysema. When you quit smoking, you become healthier, able to breathe better, and have money for new things. Smoking costs so much these days. Imagine what else you could be buying instead.

Alcohol is a depressant. Many people who drink end up crying. You may think that it is helpful, but in reality you are making yourself depressed. I am not saying to never drink, but I am saying do not drink all the time. Limit yourself. Don't drink every day or even every weekend. Not only is it making you more depressed, it is doing damage to your internal organs, also. Ever hear of cirrhosis of the liver? It causes jaundice, fatigue, and can ultimately kill you from liver failure. That's usually caused by consuming too much alcohol. It's best to limit yourself on drinking.

Recreational drugs are pulling you under. You think they help, but they keep you weighed down. You could over dose on them, too. If you are doing drugs, seek help and counselling. Check into rehab and quit. You will be so grateful you did because you will feel more alive, happier, and better.

Eliminating these habits will ultimately make you feel better, happier, and healthier.

Chapter Seven:

Relationships

I have been in extremely abusive relationships in my past. The first one was when I was eighteen and it lasted ten months. That was my worst one. He beat me, controlled me, starved me, kept me from going outside, and raped me.

The second one gradually got worse over the course of a year. He would hit me and say it was an accident. He was very controlling and wouldn't let me do anything without permission.

The third one lasted three weeks. He grabbed me up, held a gun to me, and stood over me with a knife. I knew better by the third time and got free instantly.

I have had relationships that were emotionally, mentally, and verbally abusive. This is just as bad as physical abuse. If you are in a relationship that is toxic, or abusive in any way, you need to get free. You are worth love and goodness.

I attracted these kinds of relationships by believing that in some way I deserved the mistreatment because I wasn't good enough. As soon as I realized I was good enough and deserved goodness, I attracted a kind man who has never hit me, controlled me, cussed me, or mistreated me in any way.

"We accept the love we think we deseve." Stephen Chbosky

Domestic violence is a terrible epidemic and we need to encourage victims to get free. We need to help the abusers seek counselling and get the help they need to stop the abuse.

Abuse consists of hitting, biting, spiting, slapping, kicking, punching, name calling, put-downs, controlling, shaking, starving, imprisoning, raping, cussing, yelling, choking, and manipulating.

You can get free and seek help. It is very important for your mental health to be in a healthy relationship.

A healthy relationship consists of encouragement, support, love, patience, listening, understanding, commitment, kind words, discussions, friendship, loyalty, and communication.

Being in a healthy relationship feels amazing and it helps you grow. An abusive relationship keeps you from getting better and being who you were truly meant to be.

Chapter Eight:

Changing Course

If you try something new and don't like it, the joy in life is the ability to change course. When you volunteer for something and find that it's not what you want to do, you can back out and go elsewhere.

Right now, you need to change course from your normal. You need to find what works for you. Your normal could be just staying home and not exploring your surroundings. Your course change would be to get out and discover places within your town.

You may be in a job you truly despise and hate going to. That would warrant a course change, also. You can apply at a job you may enjoy better. You won't know if you don't try.

Try new things and find what you truly enjoy doing. If I was to find that I don't like something I am doing, I would find a way to change what I am doing. You can do this, too. Life is ever-changing and nothing needs to remain permanent.

Part Six-

Things To Work On

Chapter One:

Gratitude

The first thing I started doing to get better is practicing gratitude. I started to find gratitude in the smallest things in life. My list of things I am grateful for is long.

I encourage you to make gratitude lists often. Don't leave off the basic things. Such as, breathing, food, home, clothes, love, and learning.

There are so many things to be grateful for. A beautiful sunset, a hot cup of tea, a good book, a scenic walk, and a gorgeous lake are all things to be grateful for. You can get very creative with your gratitude list.

Not only can we be grateful for all the good things in our lives, we can learn to be grateful for the darkest days, also. From every bad experience, we can find gratitude amongst the bad.

For example, think about what the bad situation taught you. We can always learn from the bad things in our lives. Every mistake is a learning possibility.

Think about what you gained from the experience. Did you gain a child that you love dearly? Did you gain a new experience? Did you happen to come across a new music genre that is now your favorite? There are many ways to find gratitude for the darkest days.

In my own life, I am grateful for my darkest days of abuse because I learned and became wise. Now, I take that wisdom and help others become better, happier, and healthier. I discovered new music during that time that I enjoy. Finally, I wrote books and got them published. Through this process, I also learned forgiveness.

Chapter Two:

Appreciation

Cultivate more appreciation in your life. Write appreciation letters to your friends and family. Learn to appreciate little joys and tiny accomplishments.

We can all appreciate the things we often take for granted. Have you told your partner that you appreciate them and all they do for you on a daily basis? Why not do that regularly?

I appreciate all the beauty and wonder in life. You can, too. By appreciating more, you can become happier. You will find new things to appreciate the more you practice.

Try to cultivate an appreciation of yourself, how great your body works, and the intricate details of what makes your body work. Our bodies are amazing. They can heal themselves, keep themselves going, and get healthier.

Appreciate all about who you are. You are a unique, awesome person just as you are. Self-appreciation cultivates self-esteem which is a vital aspect of happiness and getting better.

Chapter Three:

Fear

By doing things that scare you on a regular basis, you become less fearful. Fear holds us back so much and is very much crippling. We need to face our fears.

I mentioned act as if before. When you act like you've done something a million times and you are already prepared for it, then you perform much better. That helps prevent fear from creeping in.

Another way to prevent fear is to imagine yourself doing the activity a lot. Imagine it going very well and that will put you at ease.

Too often, we think about the scariest possible outcome. This usually never happens. Things mostly work out just fine. You need to think of the best possible outcome. You will be less fearful and more confident that way.

When we combat fear, we grow. We grow into the person we were meant to be. You can do it. Face your fears.

Chapter Four:

Forgiveness

Forgiveness is a tough subject. You need to learn to forgive every one that has ever wronged you. Forgiveness sets you free. Forgiveness does not condone the behavior. Forgiveness is not for the other person; it is ultimately for you.

When you forgive, you release all the negativity tied to the experience. It took my eight years to forgive my abusers and others in my life. Once I did, I soared. Things didn't keep me miserable anymore and I was able to grow.

I view my bad parts of my life in a positive light. I am who I am today due to what I went through. I am able to help and I am life qualified to help people become better, happier, and healthier because I had to learn how the hard way. This helped me forgive.

I wrote detailed and intricate forgiveness letters to everyone I needed to forgive and that helped me greatly. I never had to send them, but they set me free.

I can forgive anyone with these thoughts:

*What did the experience teach me?

*What did I learn?

*What good came from this situation?

*How has it made me grow?

*How can I help others from my situation?

*If they knew better, they'd do better.

These tactics always help me:

*Forgiveness letter.

*Imagine them as a sad, crying, lonely seven year old searching for love and not getting it unless you give it to them.

*Realizing all the good that came from the time.

Forgiveness is important to achieve for optimum happiness and freedom.

Chapter Five:

Confidence

Confidence helps you accomplish anything without doubts and fears. I believe that you can become more confident through action, self-esteem practices, and assertiveness training.

There is a lot that goes into building confidence. Once you have a good self-esteem and are able to assert yourself, then confidence has room to grow.

To work on self-esteem, you need to learn to love all of who you are and accept all the good and all the bad as one. You are you and that's perfect. There is nothing wrong with you. Do practices in the mirror. Tell yourself, "I love you" every time you go to the bathroom. Tell yourself, "I am good enough." Ultimately, you are good enough and deserving of all the good life has to offer you. Believe it and achieve it.

Assertiveness is being able to speak up for what you want or don't want, making eye contact, maintaining a confident posture, and believing that you deserve to be heard. Many times we have the false belief that we are unworthy or undeserving. I'm here to tell you that you are worthy! Because you are a human, you have worth and value. You are valuable. You deserve to be heard and voice your opinions. We all do. It is our birthright!

Action makes you more confident because the more you do something, the more you feel at ease doing it. Confidence comes when you believe in your self and what you are capable of doing. You can do anything you set your mind and determination to. Don't give up, ever! You can do it and once you do, your confidence will grow.

Chapter Six:

Worrying About What People Think

A lot of our worry and fear stems from us worrying about what other people think of us. We get so wrapped up in needing their acceptance and approval. What we need to do instead is, accept and approve of ourselves.

When you fully accept who you are, how you act, and the way you think, the less you care about the acceptance of others. "What other people think of you is none of your business." That is a very true quote. Why care about the thoughts of others? The only thoughts you need to worry about is your own.

Our social anxiety stems from being afraid of how others will view us. When we view ourselves with confidence, approval, and acceptance, we won't worry so much about how we are perceived.

This is a task that many people need to work on and change. It starts with cultivating approval and acceptance of yourself. The only person you need to please is yourself. Don't worry about how others are feeling about your thoughts, views, opinions, and decisions because they all have their own.

Everyone will think something different anyway. You can't worry about what they are thinking and be fully happy. You will be consumed with fear and worry over their thoughts and that's not the best way to live.

Get your own self-approval and self-acceptance without worrying about others. Some will accept you and approve of you, but many will not. Don't let that get to you or get you down. Other people's opinions should not effect you.

If other people's opinions get to you, then you must be believing what they say is true. Don't doubt yourself and gain confidence in who you are. When you do that, you'll care a lot less about their views.

Chapter Seven:

Isolation

Okay, confession time. How many of you readers isolate yourself? You avoid people and become secluded. You spend your days in your bed under your warm covers.

There was a time when I isolated myself. You know, I was very bored, lonely, and more depressed. I didn't have any one I could talk to and relate to. I was a single mother, living alone with my two young children. I lived behind websites and that was my only socializing.

This is not healthy. I needed adult socializing in my life. When I moved here and started going to church, I realized just how bad I needed friends and socializing. I laugh more, smile more, and feel better all around.

You may think you are avoiding people for a good reason. I understand. However, if you meet a toxic person, or someone you don't like, you can cut ties with them. You don't have to be their friends. You need good relationships with people who help you grow and become better.

You won't make healthy friends if you stay away from all people and isolate yourself. You need to break this habit. Leave your comfort zone. Meet new people wherever you regularly go. If you don't go anywhere, start going places. You could go to the library, join a support group, go to church, or join a club. You have many options to get out and about.

People need other people. That's how it is for optimum health, happiness, and living. You need a trusted friend you can share with and get to know well. We can all use friends.

I'm not saying surround yourself constantly with people. That would be mentally fatiguing. You do need some alone time. When you are constantly alone, that is isolation and it harms your mental health.

Part Seven-

Encouragement

Chapter One:

Positive Affirmations

Positive affirmations are helpful to our healing. You often combat negative things by positive affirmations.

We are constantly making affirmations. We are affirming what we believe. The problem is that our affirmations are usually negative.

Ex. I am not good enough.

I am fearful.

I am not safe.

They shape how we feel about ourselves and how we ultimately become. What you put after the words I am shapes your reality. Make sure they are positive.

Ex. I am healthy.

I am safe.

I am plenty good enough.

A long list of affirmations follow:

* I am beautiful.

* I am strong.

* I am determined.

* I am good.

* I am happy.

* I am good enough.

* I am bold.

* I am brave.

* I am capable.

* I am ready.

* I am willing.

* I am amazing.

* I am worth while.

* I am deserving.

Now, see how many positive affirmations you can come up with. One that I use often is: I am bold, brave, smart, wise, and in control of my own life. I am capable of making my own decisions.

Another one is: I am a bold, courageous woman who is fully capable of assertively making her own decisions. I am plenty good enough and deserving of all the good in the Universe.

My most recent favorite is: I am brave, determined, strong, and ready. I am powerful and able to live my dreams.

I encourage you to make your own special affirmations and use them daily. Think about them 10-20 times a day. Write them down and commit them to memory. They will help you in many ways. Recite them in front of a mirror for added effect. Look yourself deep in the eyes as you say I am good enough.

When you feel agitated by one, you have hit the jack pot. You want to work on that one especially because you have a deep negative affirmation that is rebelling to be let go. The less you believe in the positive affirmation, the more you need to work on it.

Chapter Two-

Helpful Quotes

The following is a list of helpful quotes that I created to help others become better, happier, and healthier.

"You are amazing exactly as you are already."

"You will accomplish your goals one step at a time."

"Every one has a chance to be happy once they know how."

"You are fully capable of accomplishiing your dreams as long as you never give up."

The following list is a list of quotes that helped me on my journey.

"Be your own kind of beautiful." Marylin Monroe

"We are all a work in progress." Unknown

"Be the change you wish to see in this world." Mahatma Ghandi

"Regret nothing because at the time, you did exactly what you wanted." Unknown

"If they knew better, they'd do better." Unknown

These are just a few of the many that I hold in my memory. There are so many inspirational quotes to choose from and discover. Search for ones that apply and inspire you on your journey to recovery.

Chapter Three:

A Special Message

You are truly capable of getting better and aquire everything you desire. Never give up hope on your dreams and wishes. Believe in yourself because you are in complete control of your mind, emotions, and feelings.

Change your negative thinking and you will open up more doors than you could ever imagine. I did. I got my books published, I am becoming a speaker, and I am making progress beyond my wildest dreams.

All it takes is a few baby steps and soon, you'll be walking miles. Dream big and don't ever let anyone tell you that you can't do something. The possibilities are endless. You got this. I believe in you and all you are capable of.

Chapter Four:

Take Your Time

Recovery isn't a race. It takes time and a lot of little steps. Do not get overwhelmed. If you begin to get overwhelmed, take a step back. It took me years to get to this point.

Follow your own agenda and don't try to do too much all at once. That will cause mayhem. Relax because you have the rest of your whole life to become better, happier, and healthier. It is a life long process. We are forever progressing and changing.

Your day will come in due time. There should not be any rushing on your part. When you are ready, you will know. When you are not ready, you will get overwhelmed and we don't want that. So, progress at a slow, even pace. Don't move on until you are completely comfortable doing the step before.

Take you time and create your own pace for the best results. Even if it takes a year or two, never give up hope. You'll get there, I promise. As long as you are trying and progressing, you will have results.

Chapter Five:

Workbooks And Journals

There are a multitude of workbooks and handbooks designed to help you get better. I use these often.

The Anxiety And Phobia Workbook by Edmund J. Bourne was very effective in my recovery. As long as you do the work, you will see fantastic results. The PTSD Workbook by Mary Beth Williams has been beneficial to me, also. I found these at the library. Have notebooks on hand so you are able to do all the exercises in the books. You must do a little mental work to get better.

Journals are out there designed to help you discover yourself and guide you along your journaling. My personal favorite journal is My 365 Day Guided Journal by Tony T. Robinson. That can be found on Amazon.com. He has other journals on Amazon as well that are worth looking into.

I highly recommend journaling, even if you simply use a notebook and write all of your inner most feelings down. You will discover more about who you are and where you want to be in your life.

Perhaps blogging is your area. You can join a blogging community and get readers to read your feelings and ramblings. I use workbooks, journals, and blogs. You can do all three or pick and choose.

Conclusion

My advice is simple. Take baby steps. Take as long as you need and you will eventually be where you were meant to be in life. Get a support system and attend a support group.

Acknowledge people. Try changing your thoughts. If you view the world as a dangerous place, view it as a safe place. It's not always dangerous all the time, right?

Be sure to see a therapist and consider medication for your own disorders. As well as medication and therapy, look in to cognitive behavioral therapy to change your thoughts.

Read many books designed to help you feel better, gain confidence, and build self-esteem. Help is out there. All you have to do is access it.

Life changes as you do. We are all a work in progress.

Contact

Website: blg2011motherof2.wix.com/author

Facebook: facebook.com/authorbrittanygunderson

Email: blg2011motherof2@yahoo.com

Blog: blg2011motherof2.wordpress.com

I have YouTube videos designed to help you become better, happier, and healthier.

Resources:

Mind Over Mood- Dennis Greenberger

Life Is Beautiful- Brittany Gunderson

The Basics Of Happiness- Brittany Gunderson

Life Loves You- Louise Hay

Be Yourself, Every One Else Is Already Taken- Mike
       Robbins

My 365 Day Guided Journal- Tony T Robinson

The Anxiety And Phobia Workbook- Edmund J. Bourne

Feeling Good- David D. Burns

The PTSD Workbook- Mary Beth Williams

Author Biography

Brittany Gunderson is a 26 years old. She is the mother of two awesome boys, Daniel and Nathan. She has a very loving and supportive boyfriend, Mike Webster. She has a few books out there. She helps people become better, happier, and healthier. She enjoys spreading domestic violence awareness and helping people.